Water

Patricia and Victor Smeltzer

A LION BOOK

Text copyright © 1984 Patricia & Victor Smeltzer
This illustrated edition © 1984 Lion Publishing

Published by
Lion Publishing plc
Icknield Way, Tring, Herts, England
ISBN 0 85648 520 9
Lion Publishing Corporation
772 Airport Boulevard, Ann Arbor, Michigan 48106, USA
ISBN 0 85648 520 9
Albatross Books
PO Box 320, Sutherland, NSW 2232, Australia
ISBN 0 86760 389 5

First edition 1984

Acknowledgements
The prayer by Elizabeth Goudge on page 30 is
used by kind permission of Gerald Duckworth and Co. Ltd.

Photographs
Sonia Halliday Photographs/Sonia Halliday: 23, 25,/Jane Taylor: 10/11;
Lion Publishing/Jon Willcocks: 2, 2/3, 5, 8/9, 11, 12 (left), 12/13,
16 (both), 17, 18 (both); South American Missionary Society; 29;
Anthea Sieveking/Vision International: 28; ZEFA: 7, 14, 15 (both),
19, 20/21, 27, 30/31.
Cover: Lion Publishing/Jon Willcocks: left above; South American
Missionary Society: right above; ZEFA: below.

British Library Cataloguing in Publication Data

Smeltzer, Patricia
    Water.
    1. Water – Moral and religious aspects –
    Juvenile literature
    I. Title   II. Smeltzer, Victor
    291.2'12   BL65.W/

    ISBN 0-85648-520-9

Printed and bound in Italy
by Poligrafici Calderara, Bologna

Contents

Water Everywhere

Over half the surface of the earth is covered with water – oceans, seas, lakes, rivers and streams.

Life on earth depends on water. All living things need water in order to exist. In fact, all plants and the bodies of all living things contain a large amount of water. Without water they would die.

Human beings and animals get water from the liquids they drink and the food they eat. Plants take in water from the ground through their roots.

Water Back to Water

As well as being *liquid*, water can be *solid*, in the form of ice or snow. It can also be invisible, as water vapour in the air.

When water on the earth's surface is warmed by the sun, some of it *evaporates* (changes to vapour) and rises into the air.

If the air cools down, some vapour changes back to tiny drops of water.

These form clouds. When the clouds grow bigger, the drops fall as rain. Sometimes they freeze and fall as hail or snow.

Most of the rain and melted snow runs into streams and rivers which flow back to the sea.

This never-ending process is known as the *water cycle*.

The Water Supply

A regular supply of water is very
important, or plants and animals and
people will die. In some parts of the world
there is plenty of water, but in others
there is not enough and water is very
precious.

People get water from streams and rivers. But there is also a hidden water supply – under the ground. Sometimes it rises to the surface as a *spring,* or people dig *wells* to get water.

People have always needed water, not only to drink, but also for their animals and crops. So wells and springs have always been important. They were often the main meeting-places, because people went there to collect water.

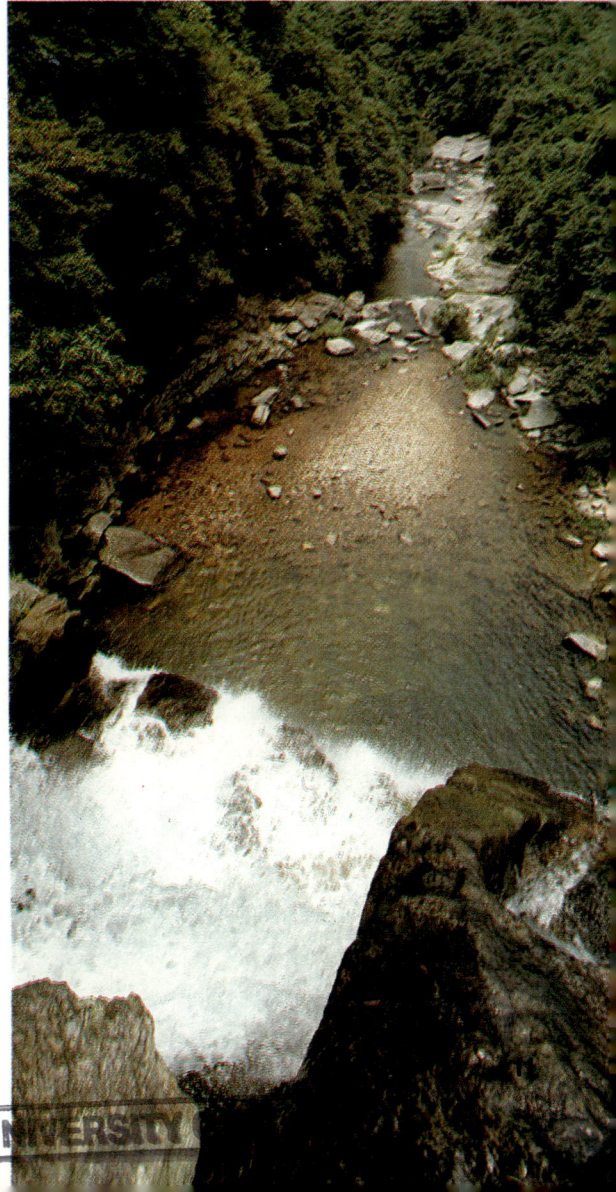

Seas and Rivers

Forests and mountains make transport difficult overland. Rivers and seas – the waterways – have always been important for carrying cargoes from one place to another, and also for carrying people.

In the past, explorers made voyages of discovery to find new lands.

Trade between different countries developed by sea. Great ports and harbours grew up.

Rivers, too, were important for communication. Towns were built on their banks, particularly where there was a crossing-place.

In the eighteenth century, before there were railways and good roads, canals were built. In some countries most of the inland transport was by canal.

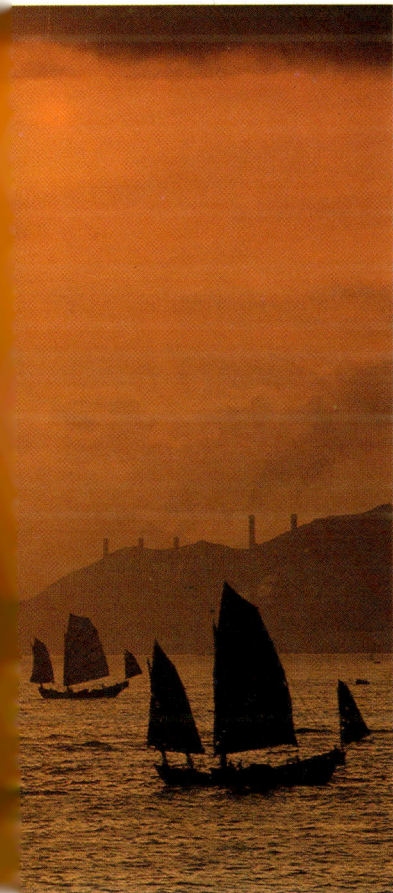

Water Works for Us

Water works for us by providing energy
– hydro-electric power
– steam turbine power
– water mills.

It works for us
– by treating sewage
– putting out fires
– cooling car engines
– at home.

Water Works for Us

In many countries people depend on fishing for food. In some countries huge trawlers go fishing the deep seas. In other countries people fish from small boats, on the sea or in rivers.

Water cleans our bodies to keep us healthy.
We use water to clean
– our homes
– our clothes
– our streets.

Leisure

Water and Life

Without water everything would die.
All over the world water is a vital part of
everyday life. We all depend on water.

Because of this, water is also a very
important part of most of the religions of
the world. Water is used as a *symbol*.
A symbol is something which stands for, or
represents, something else.

Water stands for *life* and for making things
clean.

Around the World –1

People feel they need to be made clean before they can approach God. So ritual washing plays an important part in many religions.

The great rivers of India are holy for Hindus, particularly the River Ganges, which they call 'Mother Ganga'. But the most holy place of all is Benares. Here pilgrims go down to the platforms *(ghats)* on the banks of the Ganges to wash.

At Hindu temples there are lakes or large water tanks that are used for ritual washing. On festivals and holy days the images of the Hindu gods are taken from the temples on decorated carts and bathed in the rivers.

A Hindu performs his daily prayer ceremonies at home, or on the banks of a nearby river. He takes a bath, then sprinkles water over his body.

Around the World – 2

Muslim men are called to prayer by the *muezzin* who stands at the top of a minaret (high tower) of the mosque (the Muslim place of worship).

At the entrance to the mosque is a water tank or tap. Before he can say his prayers, each man washes his hands, face, head, arms and feet. Then he enters the mosque barefoot with his head covered.

The call to prayer is made five times a day. Muslim women say their prayers at home.

Jewish people have always realized how holy and pure God is, and how much they need to be made clean to approach him. The Jews have also always had very strict rules about hygiene and cleanliness in the home.

Living Water

For Christians, water stands for new life and for being made clean.

We know that without water we would die. Jesus said, 'If anyone is thirsty, let him come to me and drink'. He was using picture-language.

Just as we all need water to live, so Jesus offers new life to everyone who believes in him. Jesus offers forgiveness for the things we have done wrong ('sins') and a new, fresh start.

Baptism

Jesus commanded that anyone who believes in him should be baptized, 'in the name of the Father, and of the Son, and of the Holy Spirit'.

Baptism with water is a sign of being spiritually clean. The first followers of Jesus were baptized in a river. This still happens in some parts of the world today. But people are also baptized inside churches. Some churches have a deep-water 'baptistry' where grown up believers are baptized.

In other churches babies are baptized by being sprinkled with water. Their parents promise to bring them up to follow Jesus.

Jesus said, 'I am the bread of life. He who comes to me will never be hungry. He who believes in me will never be thirsty.'

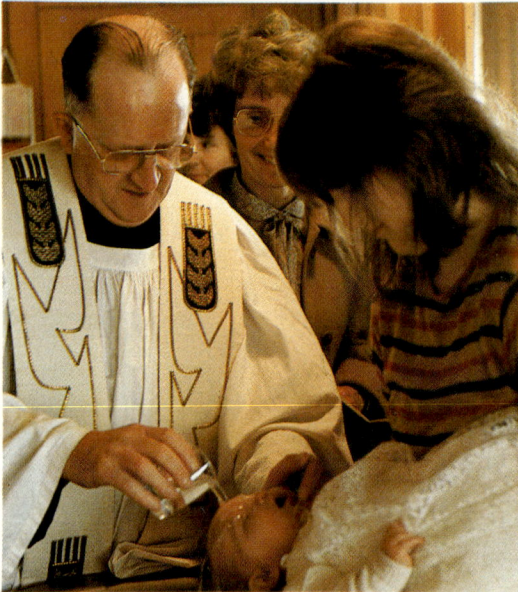

'Praised be our Lord for the wind and the rain,
For clouds, for dew and the air:
For the rainbow set in the sky above
Most precious and kind and fair.
For all these things tell the love of our Lord,
The love that is everywhere.'

Elizabeth Goudge